THE

Converted Shepherd Boy:

THE

LIFE OF JAMES RENNIE,

COLPORTEUR.

LONDON: MORGAN AND SCOTT,

(OFFICE OF "The Christian,")

12, PATERNOSTER BUILDINGS. E.C.

And may be ordered of any Bookseller.

Price One Penny.

THE

CONVERTED SHEPHERD BOY.

PART I.—DARKNESS.

" By nature the children of wrath, even as others."
EPHESIANS ii. 3.

I WAS born in Australia, about ten miles from Melbourne, at the river Plenty, on the 10th of June, 1851. My father, at the time he married, was a ploughman in Perthshire, Scotland: from there he went to Australia, to the gold diggings, to seek for the gold that perisheth. In this search he was successful. After some years he returned to Scotland, where he bought a small property in Kincardine-on-Forth, and began business as a maltster, leading John Barleycorn away from the mill to the distillery, while hundreds starved for bread.

When sober, my father was kind to his wife and children. Once our home was happy; the good old Book was read, and the voice of family prayer was heard. But then came a sad change; my father does not come home at night, but is to be found in "The Crown," with others, spending their money for that which is not bread. This is the first step; but mark what it leads to. It was a fine summer morning in the sweet month of May when father left home, as we thought, only for a few days. The time passed quickly by. We looked, but in vain, for his return. Could that loving mother think he had gone and left her with eight children to seek their way in this dark world alone? It was so; but not for some time was it found out that he had gone to America, where he was afterwards killed by an accident. How many a home has drink blighted!

Have you seen the tears of the widow and orphan, or heard the low, sad wail of agony sent up by broken hearts? Here were a mother and her family left to all appearance friendless. But bless God for a praying mother. She cried unto the Lord, who has promised to be a Father to the fatherless and a Husband to the widow; and He who has been ever faithful to His promise came to our help, and has made all things work together for good.

Nor was this all my mother had to bear at this time, for she had the grief to see her first-born son walking in evil ways. Being left to the freedom of my own will, I despised my good mother; broke the Sabbath-day, and passed it in idleness and sin, being led by Satan at his will. One sin led to another, until I became bold enough to do deeds of wickedness of which I now shudder to think. One afternoon I took a number of boys to a quarry, and we threw the workmen's barrows into the deep water. When the workmen came the next day, they had great trouble to get them out. The policeman came to me, as he often did when any mischief was done; but although we were verily guilty, lying cleared us before men.

About this time a lady offered to give me a good education. Blind to my own interest, I refused. From the first of my school-days it was a trouble to get me to go. A carter one day was asked to drive me to school: he got me into the cart and held me fast, thinking he was my master; but when on a quiet part of the road, I took my cap from my head and cast it behind the cart. He, without a thought, stopped his horse and went after it, and while so doing, I ran away. We may escape out of the hands of our fellow-men; but how shall we escape the punishment due to sin, if we neglect the "great salvation"?

Now came the time when I must leave home. Through the kindness of a few gentlemen who took an interest in our family, a situation was obtained for me at Paisley. I never can forget the trouble my mother seemed to feel on my leaving home to seek my way in the world. When I arrived at Paisley I was received with kindness, and my home was to be with the foreman over the works, a godly man. This however did not suit me; as indeed very little did in those days. The first day I went to work, it and I fell out; I went to breakfast, and went back no more that day. The Bible says that if a man will not work, neither shall he eat. (2 Thess. iii. 10.) When I got home to dinner I was locked in a room until some one came to take me to the works; I escaped by the window, and spent the remainder of the day in idleness and sin. On returning home in the evening, the foreman read the Bible to me, warning me of my danger; but it was then seed cast upon stony ground. I now respect the good man for his interest in my welfare.

After a few days' patience on my employers' part, I was sent back to my mother. But I was not allowed to stay there even one night; for the same gentleman who had obtained for me the situation at Paisley, employed a man to take me to a farmer some miles off, with a letter saying he was to do with me as he liked, and was not to allow me to come home until he had made me a better lad. I was not many days in his charge before I found myself in a barn bound hand and foot, to be lashed. Man may tame a young colt, but it takes a higher power to tame the human heart. There is a saying, "Spare the rod, and spoil the child." Let love use the rod, and then there may be good results. Thus at the early age of ten I was deep and still going deeper into sin.

After some time I was allowed to go home to see my mother, who often told me she was praying for me; and at the end of three years, when I was going to a new place, she gave me a Testament, saying, "Read this, and I will pray for you." I took the Testament, not for its worth, but out of respect to my mother. When I got to my new place the Testament was hidden away out of sight, and soon forgotten. Often, whilst herding my sheep on the moors, it might have made the time more pleasant; but I desired not the knowledge of God.

If I was forgetful of God, He was not forgetful of me, and I was led to think of the Good Shepherd by a simple thing which

happened at this time.   One hot afternoon I laid me down to
rest, and slept.   When I awoke I found all my sheep out of
the fold.   I went immediately to seek and bring them back;
but in the evening, on counting them, I found one was missing.
I sought it, but in vain.   That night, when I told my master of
the loss, he bade me go off in the morning early, and seek for
it till I found it.   I sought some weary hours before finding it.
Whilst wandering in a wood, I heard a cry, and running to the
place whence the sound seemed to come, I found the helpless
sheep among the thorns: it could do nothing but cry for help.
I cleared away the thorns, and when the sheep was let loose it
leaped for joy.   So we can do nothing to save ourselves, but
cry unto the Good Shepherd; and sometimes it is not till we
feel our need, and cry, that He comes to our aid.   Having found
us, He takes us back to His fold rejoicing; and then we are
enabled to leap for joy, as John Bunyan tells us Christian did
when he lost his burden at the foot of the cross.

> "Oh, happy day, that fixed my choice
>   On Thee, my Saviour and my God!
> Well may this glowing heart rejoice,
>   And tell its raptures all abroad.
>   Happy day, happy day,
>   When Jesus washed my sins away!"

> "I heard the voice of Jesus say,
>   'Come unto Me and rest;
> Lay down, thou weary one, lay down
>   Thy head upon My breast.'
> I came to Jesus as I was,
>   *Weary, and worn, and sad;*
> I found in Him a resting-place,
>   And He has made me glad.

> "I heard the voice of Jesus say,
>   'Behold, I freely give
> The living water; thirsty one,
>   Stoop down, and drink, and live.'
> I came to Jesus, and I drank
>   Of that life-giving stream;
> My thirst was quenched, my soul revived,
>   And now I live in Him."

Part II.—LIGHT.

"That ye put off the old man . . . and that ye put on the new man."
Ephesians iv. 22, 24.

The good old Book says, that if we seek God early we shall find Him. (Prov. viii. 17.) We may be too late in seeking for pardon, but we never can be too early. At the age of sixteen God began the work of grace in my heart. It was in the year 1867, in the month of June, on the first Sabbath in the month. When I awoke that morning the sun was shining brightly, though my soul was dark and full of sin : two companions of mine had gone to see their friends, and so I was left alone. But God was drawing near while I sat in the house. Thought after thought crossed my mind as I recalled my past life. What a sinner I had been ! My conscience was troubled, and for the first time I thought of my mother's prayers and the Testament she gave me when leaving home, and which afterwards I had hidden away. I now sought it out; but in it I could see no word to give my mind ease : it was to me a sealed book. To get rid of gloomy thoughts, I went out into a field of grass to sleep them off. But there is no rest for the wicked. Away from God! and how can I get to Him? If I remained in the City of Destruction I must perish. Evangelist, where art thou? Not far off, when a soul is in trouble of this kind.

As the day was passing, I heard of a meeting that was to be held at the next farm, and determined to go. The preacher was a poor collier with little knowledge in his head, but much of God's love in his heart; he told in burning words what a sinner he had been, a drunkard, a sabbath-breaker, and yet that God had saved him. "Then," thought I, "there is hope for me, even me." Soon my heart was melted, and my cheeks were wet with tears. The people looked at me in my trouble, and remarked, "What a fool he is." They were right, I had been a fool indeed; but Christ was about to put me in my right mind. What the world thought of me I cannot tell; all I had in myself was corruption and death.

But weeping could not save me. The preacher came to me in my trouble, and said,

"Do you feel you are a sinner?"

I answered, "If ever a man did, I do."

"Then," he said, "Christ is a Saviour for you."

> "'Just as you are, without one plea,
> But that the blood was shed for thee.'"

I walked with the preacher on the road home that evening: we sat down together under the branches of a spreading tree, and before I left that spot I was made, by God's grace, a new man in Christ Jesus. Some may say, "How did you find peace?" I answer, "Only in believing!" I first saw myself to be a sinner, and then Christ as a Saviour. The preacher spoke to me like this: "Salvation is too cheap for you; it is too simple. You would like to buy it; but God gives it for nothing." He continued, "Look up to heaven, and say, Christ is yours, and you are His; and you will find peace." And, glory be to God, I looked up to heaven with the eye of faith; like a drowning man struggling for life. I said, "Christ is mine, and I am His." Hark! the angels are singing over the poor shepherd-boy being born again; and there is not only joy in heaven, but in my soul also; yes, a "joy unspeakable and full of glory."

I had now entered in at the strait gate. The preacher said, "It is for you to keep the light of the cross in view, and run towards the prize. Look up when tempted; Jesus reigns and pleads for thee." And so we parted.

It was late when I reached home, and my two companions were fast asleep. My soul was full of joy; and, like the woman who found her piece of silver, and said to her neighbours, "Come and rejoice with me," I thought they would be glad to hear that I had found the "Pearl of great price." But I soon found out they were like the elder son of old, who would not rejoice at the return of his brother; they were angry, and said I was surely going mad.

"Oh no," I said,

> "Jesus makes me glad;
> Bless His name:

"and I am going home."

Guilty sinner, will you come or not? An awful doom is hovering over you.

> "Farewell! I will not go with you to hell:
> I mean with Jesus Christ to dwell.
> Will you go?"

If a man is made right inside, you will see also a great change outside. I had, as it were, been turned from a lion into a lamb; the lips that before cursed God, now tried to bless Him.

A few days after this I went home to see my praying mother. I had not been in the house five minutes before she saw the change. I did not need to tell her what had happened, for in my face the hope of glory beamed; and it was with joy I went to the old Kirk, and found it to be the gate of heaven to my soul.

When first brought to a knowledge of the truth, I could read but very little; but the old saying is true, "Where there's a will there's a way." The long-hidden Testament became my constant companion; and after eleven years up and down, over hills and dales, I can sing:

> "Oh, good old way, how sweet thou art!
> May none of us from thee depart;
> But may our actions always say,
> 'We are hastening on the good old way.'"

I may have many miles to travel before I reach the home beyond; still, the Captain of our salvation says, "I am with you alway, even unto the end of the world." (Matt. xxviii. 20.) If we keep trusting to such a Guide, we may go forth fearing no evil, for He that is with us is mightier than all that can be against us.

It is my desire to get others to go with me to the better

country. Christ took with Him a poor thief; it is our duty to follow the Master's example. When I sent forth the first edition of this little narrative, it was in the hope that God would bless it to some soul; for "it is not by might, nor by power, but by My Spirit, saith the Lord." And God *has* in many instances blessed it to the end intended. Here is one.

A poor woman in the village of S—— had a copy, and sent it to her son, a soldier in India. Some time afterwards the mother came to me with tears of joy, saying her son had sent her a letter, stating that the little book about the *Converted Shepherd Boy* had been blessed to his soul's salvation.

Another instance. One evening, whilst speaking to the people of D——, I was sent for to go and see a young woman who was very ill. I went, and found her in great trouble about her soul. I asked her what brought on her trouble of mind. She said she had been reading the account of my early life, and it led her back to sins of the same kind, which had been forgotten by her, but not forgiven by God; and she could not rest until Christ forgave her all. Two years after, when I was standing in Bedford Market with my book-stall, a well-dressed young woman came up, and after a little talk it turned out that she was the same young person whom I had visited at the village of D——. I was rejoiced that she thus came and acknowledged the mercy of God in saving her soul.

If these were the only two cases, then bless God for them! But I could tell of many more; and the day is coming when sower and reaper will see the full fruits of their labours. It is for us to labour on in God's strength: whatsoever our hands find to do, let us do it with all our might.

It is with such encouragement, and under a demand for more copies, that I send forth a new edition with the same end in view as at first—salvation of souls and the glory of God.

PART III.—WORK.

"Son, go work to-day in my vineyard."—MATT. xxi. 28.

MY call to colportage work.

It was whilst I was a member of the "Alloa Young Men's Christian Association" that the secretary received a letter from the late Rev. William Boyd, of the Scottish Tract and Book Society, Edinburgh, saying they wanted some earnest young men as colporteurs. Several applied, and were received. I was told by one or two of the elder members to apply, as they thought it was a work for which I should be well suited. I thought differently, and had many reasons for doing so; but after some pressing by friends, I prayed over it. I sent five testimonials from ministers and other gentlemen; and after passing all examinations, I was told that a colporteur was wanted in Bedfordshire.

The thought of leaving home and kind friends made me hesitate at the journey of some four hundred miles, till I thought of Him who came from heaven's highest height to earth's lowest home to work out my salvation. I felt that if Christ did so much for me, it could not be too much for me to leave all and follow Him. So I bade farewell for a season to those at home, and took steamer from Leith to London. I was not long on board ship before I began the good work, giving away tracts, and selling books not a few—one to a young couple newly married, called, *Happy homes, and how to make them happy.*

When I arrived at Bedford I thought of John Bunyan, who had travelled life's rough way before me. Here I met Mr. B——, who received me with kindness, and instructed me to go on to Biggleswade, my first field of public labour. The first night I saw something of what Biggleswade was like, and how far some were living from God. If there is a time when a young man needs help from above, it is when he is leaving home, going into the world of temptation and sin. Had not the Lord been on my side I must have fallen; but His grace is sufficient for us. During my four and a half years of labour in that district I had my times of trouble; but let them go to the wind when they had taught their lessons. I must say, after all, " the lines have fallen unto me in pleasant places;" for God has made all things work together for good.

You may ask what was done during these four and a half years in the colportage work. I sold over £2000 worth of Bibles and pure literature, in number over 100,000 volumes, and nearly 300,000 periodicals; these, with thousands of tracts, have been taken into more than thirty villages, and but for this agency they would never have found their way to the homes of the people. I have been told that it is a mistake for working people to buy books; but I say books are better than beer, and the reading of these books has, with God's blessing, made many a sober, thoughtful father and son, mother and daughter, while beer has brought many to shame and ruin. Books instead of beer! and we shall have more peace in our homes, and more people to our churches and chapels.

Many in my old district bless the day that this work was begun. The good reading has made many a working man's heart happier and the day brighter. I crave for no lighter work than this. It has been said it is a work second to none. It is a work of God, blessed by Him to the salvation of souls.

The following are a few of the kinds of books sold : Over 3000 Bibles and Testaments, 1200 *Sunday Readings*, 1000 *Golden Treasury*, 1500 Bunyan's works, 800 *Young Man from Home*, 600 *Bright Examples*, 500 *Dairyman's Daughter*, 400 *Weighty Words*, 200 *Early Piety*, 200 *Blood of Jesus*, 130 *God's Way of Peace*, 500 *Billy Bray*, 2000 *Songs and Solos*, 100 *The Bible and Working People*. Thousands of similar works have been sold at reduced prices, and many large Family Bibles, which are treasured in the homes.

If we sow good seed we may, with God's blessing, expect a good harvest.

" We are sowing, ever sowing,
　Something good or something ill ;
In the lives of those around us
　We are planting what we will.

" Not a word we say falls fruitless,
　Not a deed we do decays ;
Every thought and word and action
　Will be found in future days.

" When perhaps the hand that sowed them
　Shall itself have ceased to be,
Still the record of their being
　Will live on eternally.

" Grant then, Lord of all the harvest,
　That the daily seeds we sow
May refresh the hearts of others,
　Spreading blessing as they grow."

Colportage work is one, like many others, in which a man needs grace, patience, and courage ; for although it is a good work, all do not think well of it. Some because they do not understand its object ; others because they do. I called upon a minister once, and the first thing he said was, that he did not believe in our work ; but it was because he, like many others, knew not its object, and before I left the gentleman he was a little more in favour of it. If it be a work of any good, we cannot expect all men to speak well of it. So it is for us to labour on in the strength of the great Master, rejoicing in the thought that He who is for us is mightier than all who can be against us.

By the liberality of Christian friends, the good work has been begun in my new and central district, Hitchin. This town and neighbourhood is much in need of such a work, for here can be seen a number of all ages sitting together who earn their bread by plaiting ; and as it is a work needing but little attention of the mind, many are to be found singing songs, not of Zion, but of earth's dreams, or reading such literature as would corrupt the minds of the fairest and purest.

I am happy to say that during the past year twenty villages, sometimes more, have been visited monthly, and in these villages in twelve months have been sold 5000 volumes of books, 7000 periodicals, 3000 tracts and *Monthly Visitors*, 1000 copies of *Colportage Almanacks*, 350 *Band of Hope Almanacks*, with about 4000 tracts distributed free. So in many of these homes are now to be found books and papers that are instructive, amusing, and truthful. Yet after all that has been done there remains much more to be done; for in many a home where there is a large family very few volumes are to be seen. I have been told ofttimes not to work too hard or I shall stock the people and lose my place; but if I live to be a good old age it will take me all my time to do that.

Sometimes it is a trouble to get the people to look into my box. While passing through a village for the first time, the people stared, and I heard one say to another, "That man has got watches and earrings I daresay." I brought forth a six-penny Bible, saying, "Buy this and use it aright; it is the best sword to fight the Evil One with." I sold among the said people, through those few words, several books. So I go forth day by day, carrying good news to all.

A colporteur may be called the heavenly postman; for many a message from God is in the books, messages that have been blessed to the salvation of souls, the building up of saints, and the cheering of those in trouble.

Besides carrying forth the written Word, I can tell of its power to save. During the year I have been enabled to conduct over forty meetings in the villages.

"I WILL BLESS THE LORD AT ALL TIMES : HIS PRAISE SHALL CONTINUALLY BE IN MY MOUTH."

PART IV.—COLPORTAGE.

"And from house to house."—ACTS xx. 20.

JOTTINGS FROM MY NOTE BOOK.

In the last two months I have sold over 200 *Children's Treasury*, and *Infant's Delight*, illustrated books, reduced to sixpence. They are doing a good work; many of the children meet me on the road and repeat sweet pieces out of them. My heart warms to the little ones.

God's smile is on the work. The Rev. —— gives great help in his parish. He says he will subscribe next year. Through him, Lady ——, of —— Park, asked some old women to tell me to call at the "big house." I did so, and saw her ladyship. She asked many questions about the work, which seemed to gladden her. I have to call again. Thank God for the "honourable women" of every class.

I think it would be well to attend some of the country fairs; shepherds, cowmen, and boys are very accessible on these occasions.

My district being large, I should like more tracts, good, illustrated, unsectarian tracts, well got-up; also some fly-leaves for the young. The little children take a great interest in the work, and it is always a pleasure to let them look at the contents of the pack, even when they cannot buy.

Met a poor man on the road, just out of the workhouse, where he had spent the night. Walked together for three miles to P——. He had nothing in the world, but could speak of the goodness of God to him. Gave him a small book, *The Blood of Jesus*, and half my dinner.

It is often difficult to get away from the dear good people in my district; their kindness is great. It is very often, "Come in and have something to eat, or a cup of tea." Forgot to take out my usual bread and cheese one day, and found I could have had dinner in half a dozen places, but did not do so: waited till three p.m., when I had tea with an old friend.

I often call upon the Rev. ——, who has been a true and staunch friend since the commencement. Much work is being done at his chapel.

Often tired in the work, but never weary of it. By taking the first morning train to some adjacent station, it gives me a better chance of a full day's work. I hope the Society will not grudge the additional expense incurred, as it enables us to overtake more villages.

At S—— rectory, the Rev. —— and Mrs. —— have bought largely last month to give to the poor. They rejoice in the colportage work, and I have met with great kindness and much encouragement from them. The rector says he loves every one who loves the Lord Jesus.

Visited —— Infirmary with tracts and books.

An old man told me he had been converted under the preaching of Legh Richmond one Good Friday in Turvey Church, and that the memory of the good old pastor is still cherished. One Sunday night, when Mr. R—— had been preaching, his house was broken into. The culprit proved to be a youth who had been in the Sunday-school, but had taken to bad ways. He was sent to prison, and the minister met him when he came from jail, and drove him home in his gig; got him employment, and set him on the right road. The boy told his widowed mother that but for this she would never have seen him again.

At ——, the schoolmistress burned the leaflets I gave to the children, saying "they were chapel tracts." I called and was able to satisfy her a little more.

Received with favour at —— Rectory, and also by the Wesleyans. They appear to work happily together.

Met six navvies on tramp on their way from Dover, going to work at Nottingham. Read to them, and gave them a tract each. They were very attentive, and expressed their thanks. I see the poor often help the poor; these navvies gave something to eat to a poor half-starved looking man whom they passed on the road.

London : Morgan and Scott, 12, Paternoster Buildings, E.C.